Andrew Dickson White

Outlines of Lectures on History

Addressed to the Students of the Cornell University

Andrew Dickson White

Outlines of Lectures on History

Addressed to the Students of the Cornell University

ISBN/EAN: 9783337203726

Printed in Europe, USA, Canada, Australia, Japan

Cover: Foto ©Thomas Meinert / pixelio.de

More available books at **www.hansebooks.com**

OUTLINES

OF

LECTURES ON HISTORY

ADDRESSED TO THE STUDENTS

OF

THE CORNELL UNIVERSITY

BY

ANDREW D. WHITE
PRESIDENT, AND PROFESSOR OF HISTORY

ITHACA
THE UNIVERSITY PRESS
MDCCCLXXXIII

CONTENTS.

I. FRANCE BEFORE THE REVOLUTION.

UNITY AND CENTRALIZATION.

THE REFORMATION AND WARS OF RELIGION.

HENRY IV.

THE ADMINISTRATION OF RICHELIEU.

THE ADMINISTRATION OF MAZARIN.

ST. VINCENT DE PAUL.

LOUIS XIV.

BOSSUET AND FENELON.

THE REGENCY AND LOUIS XV.

FRENCH INSTITUTIONS BEFORE THE REVOLUTION.

THE FRENCH PHILOSOPHERS OF THE XVIIIth CENTURY.

THE SUPPRESSION OF THE JESUIT ORDER.

LOUIS XVI.

TURGOT.

THE INFLUENCE OF AMERICAN IDEAS UPON THE FRENCH REVOLUTION.

II. THE FRENCH REVOLUTION.

TO THE FORMATION OF THE NATIONAL ASSEMBLY.

TO THE STORMING OF THE BASTILLE.

CONTENTS.

TO THE ABOLITION OF FEUDAL PRIVILEGES.
TO THE REMOVAL OF THE KING TO PARIS.
TO THE FEDERATION FESTIVAL.
TO THE CLOSE OF THE NATIONAL ASSEMBLY.
TO THE OUTBREAK OF THE WAR WITH EUROPE.
TO THE INSURRECTION OF THE TENTH OF AUGUST.
TO THE BEGINNING OF THE NATIONAL CONVENTION.
TO THE EXECUTION OF THE GIRONDISTS.
TO THE DOWNFALL OF ROBESPIERRE.
TO THE DIRECTORY.

III. MODERN FRANCE.

THE DIRECTORY—TO THE TREATY OF CAMPO FORMIO.
—— —TO THE EIGHTEENTH BRUMAIRE.
THE CONSULATE.
THE FIRST EMPIRE—TO THE TREATY OF TILSIT.
—— —TO THE CONFERENCE AT ERFURT.
—— —TO THE INVASION OF RUSSIA.
—— —TO THE ABDICATION OF NAPOLEON.
THE RESTORATION.
LOUIS PHILIPPE.
THE REPUBLIC OF 1848 AND THE SECOND EMPIRE.
THIERS.
THE THIRD REPUBLIC.

UNITY AND CENTRALIZATION.

1. *Europe at the End of the Middle Ages:*—Similarity in internal condition and development of the great nations,—decline of feudalism and growth of centralization,—in England,—in Spain,—in Italy,—in Germany,—in France.

2. *Condition of France:*—The Hundred Years' War and its results. Insubordination of the nobles,—their leagues and lawlessness. The military system,—evils of the feudal method,—ravages of the soldiery. The common people,—sentiments of the nobility toward them,—their misery,—war, famine, and pestilence. The Church,—noble work of the spirit of Christianity,—baneful effects of ecclesiasticism,—light thrown by the history of that age upon certain ecclesiastical hopes and promises in this.

3. *Charles VII (1422–61):*—Jeanne d'Arc and the expulsion of the English. Importance of the year 1453 to Europe and to France,—end of the Hundred Years' War. Formation of the first standing army,—its size,—importance of the step. Revenues of the crown,—the *taille*,—it is made perpetual,—significance of this. Creation of new provincial parliaments, or royal courts of appeal,—beginnings of a uniform code. Improvements in finance,—Jacques Cœur. Dealings with the Church,—the Pragmatic Sanction of 1438.

4. *Louis XI (1461–83):*—Hopes of the nobility,—declaration of Dunois,—their disappointment,—power and pretentions of some of them,—the dukes of Burgundy and Brittany. Character of Louis. Authorities upon his reign,—Philippe de Comines,—Walter Scott. Louis's

policy,—the "League of the Public Good" and its defeat,—Louis's methods illustrated by his dealings with Liége. Dealings with Burgundy,—character of Charles the Bold and of his court,—his destruction through Louis's intrigues. Ability in administration shown in selection of state servants,—in creation of new parliaments,—in dealings with the Church and with ecclesiastics (Cardinal Balue and his cage),—contrast between Louis's public and personal relations with the Church. His agency in general progress,—printing,—the post,—institutions of learning,—curious exception in his treatment of the Nominalists. Summary of his work.

5. *Charles VIII (1483–98)*:—Revolt of the nobles,—wretched condition of the people. The expedition into Italy (1494),—its real significance, according to Guizot,—its important results to Europe,—beginning of international relations. Results to France,—growth of a national consciousness,—effects of the expedition upon French character and French art.

6. *Louis XII (1498–1515)*:—External affairs,—continued interference in Italy,—rise of the idea of the "balance of power,"—the League of Cambray and the Holy League. Internal affairs,—growth of the parliaments and of procedure,—of postal communication,—of art, especially architecture. Good influence of Louis's personal character upon the nation,—its uniqueness in this respect,—Francis I, Henry IV, and Louis XIV as examples of the contrary.

THE REFORMATION AND WARS OF RELIGION.

1. *The Reform Party in France:*—Premature ideas of reform in Southern France in the 13th century,—establishment of the Inquisition, and utter extirpation of the Albigensian heresy. The Protestant Reformation,—beginnings at Meaux,—Briçonnet,—Lefèvre,—Farel,—Calvin and his work. Effect of popular discontent in inducing the rural population to accept the new doctrines,—similar effect of the supremacy of the Medici and the Guises at court upon certain high nobles. Reform sympathies of a large body of thoughtful men and women,—Marguerite of France. Selfish motives of sundry nobles.

2. *The Church Party:*—The court,—peculiar union of churchmanship with immorality,—attitude of Francis I (1515-47).

3. *Beginnings of Government Dealings with Heterodoxy:*—Arguments for intolerance. Persecution of the Vaudois,—terrible severity of Oppède. Remorse of the king,—struggle of his better instincts in the case of Berquin,—execution of Berquin. New persecutions,—torture of the heretics,—declaration of the king.

4. *Henry II (1547-59):*—His character,—execution of Anne Dubourg. Character of the queen, Catherine de Medici. Death of Henry.

5. *Catherine de Medici and Her Sons:*—Francis II (1559-60). Continued persecutions,—growth of the reform party,—Protestant conspiracy of Amboise,—its failure and cruel retribution. Charles IX (1560-74). Attempts at agreement,—colloquy of Poissy,—Beza and Lainez,—manifest futility of this effort. Attempts at toleration,—the chancellor L'Hôpital,—Bodin and Castelnau,

—growing bitterness of party spirit. Outbreak of civil war,—the outrage at Vassy,—popularity of Francis of Guise,—his assassination,—the war begun.

6. *The Three Factions :*—1. The Catholic party,—the Guises,—their mixed motives,—popular element in the party. 2. The Huguenot party,—its strongholds,—Coligny and the Bourbons. 3. The moderate party,—L'Hôpital and Bodin,—its aims. Incapacity of the Valois kings to control the struggle,—their policy.

7. *The Massacre of St. Bartholomew (1572):*—Attempt at reconciliation by marriage of Henry of Navarre with Marguerite of Valois,—invitation of all the great Protestants to the wedding,—the marriage festivities. The plot,—the king's reluctant consent,—St. Bartholomew's Day (24 Aug. 1572),—murder of Coligny,—the massacre,—frenzy of the king,—cunning purpose of Catherine de Medici. The flowering hawthorn,—renewal of the massacre,—its spread throughout France,—its extent, —immediate and remote results. Reception of the news throughout Europe,—in England,—at Rome. Responsibility of the Church.

8. *The Wars of the League :*—Escape and recantation of Henry of Navarre. Formation of the *Holy League*,—its leaders and abettors. Difficult position of Henry III (1574–89) and his court,—traditional Valois policy of trimming. Efforts to keep up fanaticism,—the "Sixteen," —curious parallel between these methods and those of the English Puritans. Efforts to secure aid from abroad,—sympathies of the several powers. Increase of the popularity of the Guises,—Day of the Barricades (1588),—desperation of Henry III,—the Guises assassinated at Blois. Fury of the Catholic party,—assassination of Henry III by Jacques Clément (1589).

9. *Effects of the Reformation and Wars of Religion :*—On the physical condition of the French people,—on their intellectual development,—on their moral development,—on their political development. The great want of France.

HENRY IV.

1. *State of France after the Assassination of Henry III:* —Condition of Paris,—bitterness of preachers, monks, and people,—their insane hatred of Henry of Navarre. Condition of the provinces,—turbulence of the nobles,—efforts of the cities. Claimants to the crown,—Henry of Navarre and the Salic law,—Philip of Spain,—the Cardinal de Bourbon,—the young duke of Guise. Disadvantage to Henry of his Protestantism.

2. *Henry's Struggle against Force:*—Opposition of the Church,—of Spain,—of factions in France. Elements of strength in Henry,—his early life,—his home training,—his mother, Jeanne d'Albret,—his favorite reading in boyhood,—lesson of this as to the uses of biography,—influence of the Lives of the Saints and of Plutarch's Lives, as illustrations,—results in Henry's case,—Moncontour. His character,—curious mixture of qualities,—his religious spirit,—his frank, attractive manner,—his loose ideas as to morality,—his shrewdness. Points in his favor,—his legitimacy,—its recognition by his predecessor,—his military success,—his valor,—Arques and Ivry. Insane energy of the League in Paris,—fanaticism and atrocities of the mob, —result of all this.

3. *His Struggle against Opinion:*—Change in popular feeling toward him,—reaction in his favor at Paris,—his personal efforts to this end,—his sayings,—his kindly acts. The *Satire Ménippée*,—its authors,—its popularity,—plan

of the work (citations). Henry's conversion to Catholicism [1593],—his coronation,—his entrance into Paris [1594]. Union of the nation in the war against Spain,—Peace of Vervins [1598].

4. *His Religious Policy:*—Religious condition of France,—political necessity of Henry's conversion,—arguments in its favor. Conditions of his absolution,—readmission of the Jesuits. Feeling of earnest Protestants, like Duplessis-Mornay and D'Aubigné. The *Edict of Nantes* [1598],—its nature,—guaranties for its execution,—political danger of this granting of strongholds. Comparison of the Edict of Nantes with the Religious Peace of Augsburg.

5. *His Foreign Policy:*—His dealings with the House of Austria,—his plan for a great new European state-system, as laid down in Sully's memoirs,—doubtful authenticity of this.

6. *His Domestic Policy:*—Mixture in his statesmanship of thoughtfulness and carelessness. His magnanimity. *Sully*,—his character,—his ideas and reforms,—his theory as to agriculture,—Olivier de Serres and his book. Henry's noble encouragement of manufactures,—his faith in free trade. His public works,—canals,—palaces,—the cathedral of Orleans. His dealings with the nobles,—his lenience,—their lawless independence,—dueling,—D'Épernon and Biron,—execution of the latter.

7. *His Colonial Policy:*—The French in America,—De Monts and Champlain,—Quebec.

8. *The New Growth of Fanaticism:*—Preparations for war with Spain,—assassination of Henry by the Jesuit Ravaillac [1610].

THE ADMINISTRATION OF RICHELIEU.

1. *Statesmanship:*—Three leading types of statesmanship. 1. That based on faith in some great militant principle,—Cavour, Cobden, Lincoln, Sumner. 2. That which reorganizes an old state to fit new times,—Cranmer, Turgot, Gladstone. 3. That which serves a state in times of chaos,—Richelieu.

2. *France in Distress:*—Death of Henry IV. [1610],—first phase of national feeling,—second phase. Clutch by the nobles at power,—D'Épernon and the Parliament of Paris. Regency of Marie de Medici,—the Concinis,—troubles from the great nobles,—their last threat. States-General finally called [1614],—complaints of the nobles,—of the clergy,—of the people,—France as pictured in Miron's speech,—the sessions stopped ridiculously. What had been given to France,—remembrances of young Richelieu's speech. Condé and the nobles defiant again,—Richelieu given control of the kingdom,—his dealings with the rebellion. Catastrophe which throws him out of power,—end of the Concinis,—De Luynes,—formidable organization of the Protestants,—civil war again,—Richelieu recalled. Picture of France at this period, from Richelieu's *Testament Politique,*—three great objects of Richelieu's policy of which he was conscious,—one great object of which he was unconscious.

3. *Richelieu and the Huguenots:*—Position of the Huguenots in La Rochelle,—skill of Richelieu's diplomacy,—

boldness of his attack. The check,—Buckingham and the English,—their failure. Heedlessness of the nobles,—Richelieu erects new siege-works,—builds his dyke,—forms a new navy,—reforms the army,—outwits traitors,—subdues the king and court. Desperate courage of the Huguenots. Richelieu's greatness after victory.

4. *Richelieu and the Great Nobles:*—His point of attack,—first lesson to the grandees,—second lesson,—was Richelieu cruel? Hatred,—new lessons to nobles,—lesson to the Parliament of Paris. Richelieu calls in the aid of the people,—the Assembly of Notables,—reforms.

5. *Richelieu and Austria:*—Striking peculiarity of Richelieu's European alliances. His relations with German Protestants,—Father Joseph's work. The masterstroke.

6. *Summary of Richelieu's Work:*—1. On the political progress of France. 2. On the general progress of Europe. 3. On the secularization of European politics. 4. On the internal prosperity of France. Light thrown on his life at his hour of death.

THE ADMINISTRATION OF MAZARIN.

1. *Kingship:*—The search for it,—nominal kings,—real kings. Death of Richelieu [1642],—his grasp on France not relaxed,—death of Louis XIII. [1643],—*his* grasp on France relaxed at once. Will of the dead Louis broken by his friends,—wish of the dead Richelieu obeyed by his enemies,—reason of this.

2. *Mazarin:*—His training,—his character,—comparison of Mazarin with Richelieu. Glance at the military history of his administration,—the Thirty Years' War,—the Peace of Westphalia [1648].

3. *Ferment:*—Civil history, 1641-48,—Mazarin's preliminary smoothness,—he carries out Richelieu's policy,—ferment among the *nobles*. Great fault of statesmen in that age,—D'Émeri,—ferment among the *people*. The Parliament of Paris,—its character and career,—its resistance to Mazarin and D'Émeri,—influence of the English revolution,—Mazarin resolves to humble the Parliament,—the Paulette,—the Parliament humbles Mazarin,—the twenty-seven articles,—ferment in the *Parliament*. Cardinal de Retz,—his character and schemes. Summary of the situation.

4. *Explosion:*—The *Te Deum* for the victory of Lens,—seizure of Broussel,—hubbub,—Mazarin forced to yield,—the Treaty of St. Germain [1648].

5. *The Fronde:*—Mazarin's new move,—De Retz's new rebellion,—siege of Paris,—broad farce,—the new

nickname. De Retz and the nobles go too far,—the Parliament, frightened, treats with Mazarin (Peace of Rueil, 1649). The rebellion degenerates,—confusion of petty motives,—Beaufort's skill in teasing Mazarin. Complexity of the plot,—fickleness and treachery of the actors,—Mazarin alone persistent,—his exile. Mazarin returns from exile,—his triumph [1653].

6. *Absolutism built at last:*—Last struggle of the Parliament,—Mazarin teaches young Louis XIV to crush it. First need of France at that time,—fate of unearnest nations,—comparison of the Fronde with the English revolution. Mazarin's policy. Summary of the effects wrought out by Richelieu and Mazarin.

ST. VINCENT DE PAUL.

1. *Sources:*—Four great historical currents which attract notice,—one current which escapes notice,—its origin and course,—growths which it has nourished,—the most beautiful of these. The soil,—vileness of French life at the beginning of the seventeenth century, as shown by the history of that period,—noble position of one man in that history and in all history,—real secret of the power of the Church of Rome.

2. *Vincent de Paul* [*1576–1660*]:—His birth and early life,—his education,—his orthodoxy,—his dislike of theologic disputes. Strange story of his captivity and escape,—his rise into prominence,—curious connection with Cardinal de Retz. He is found by his life-work.

3. *His Work:*

A.—*St. Vincent and the Clergy:*—Condition of the French clergy in his time. His efforts for their improvement,—his personal influence,—his seminaries,—his new religious order (the Priests of the Mission). Official recognition,—the Council on Religious Affairs,—reason of its dissolution.

B.—*St. Vincent and the Afflicted:*—1. His work with the peasantry,—wretched sanitary condition of Europe,—growth of the new charity,—efforts to relieve the misery brought by war. 2. The Sisters of Charity,—first suggestion of the order,—its growth from his heart,—its wonderful spread. 3. His work among criminals,—story regarding his devotion to the galley-slaves. 4. His work for the foundlings,—his asylums,—anecdotes of his love for these helpless waifs,—hold taken by this upon the popular heart, as shown by representations of him in painting and sculpture.

4. *His Character:*—Its development,—his submission to Church authority,—his ascetic habits,—his rare combination of the deepest religious feeling with great administrative ability,—Vincent de Paul and John Wesley.

5. *His Relations to the Political History of his Time:* —1. His tutelage of De Retz. 2. His influence with the queen in favor of the retention of Mazarin. Great moral truth revealed by his relations with Richelieu and Mazarin.

6. *His Beatification and Canonization:*—His self-devotion and its natural result,—illustration of this result at the death of Louis XIII. Miracles ascribed to him,—inevitableness of this ascription. Beginning of proceedings for his beatification [1712],—preliminary testimony,—examination of his body,—formal investigation of the miracles,—defeat of the "Devil's Advocate",—papal decree of beatification [1729]. Popular rejoicings over this event,—multiplication of miracles,—taking of additional testimony,—the Pope's approval of the two required miracles,—the bill of canonization [1737]. Reality of Vincent's saintship.

LOUIS XIV.

FIRST LECTURE.

I. The Fronde and the Young King.

1. *Effect of the Fronde* on Louis's character,—lessons which it taught him,—conviction and theory which it gave him.

2. *Influence of Mazarin* on Louis's education,—Mazarin's prophecy regarding him,—first public revelation of his qualities. Death of Mazarin [1661],—his two legacies to Louis. Louis reigns alone,—character of his rule.

II. Fertility of the Time in Great Men.

1. *Colbert:*—His career,—vast scope of his activity. A. *Colbert and Finance:* Chaos,—Fouquet,—Colbert's unpopularity and its causes,—his taxation of luxuries,—his hostility to loans,—improvement of the revenue during his administration. B. *Colbert and Agriculture:* His good work at the outset,—his great fault in policy,—protection. C. *Colbert and Manufactures:* Suppression of holidays,—other fostering measures,—protection again,—France and Holland. D. *Colbert and the Navy.* E. *Colbert and the Fine Arts.* Disgrace and death of Colbert [1683],—end of the peaceful period of Louis's reign.

2. *Louvois and War:*—His skill in directing armies,—his faculty for organization,—his faults.

3. *Vauban and Military Engineering:*—His improvements in the art of fortification,—in the art of besieging.

4. *Séguier and Legislation:*—The new codification,—the six codes.

5. *De Lionne, D'Avaux, and Bonrepaux in Diplomacy:*—Their wonderful skill,—Louis's stupid vanity.

6. *Other Great Men:*—Generals.—Poets.—Prose-writers.— Philosophers.— Pulpit-orators.— Historians. — Men of learning.—Painters.—Sculptors.—Architects.

7. *Cause of this Blaze of Genius and Talent:*—Whence came these great men?—"Which is the more favorable to the development of art, science, and literature—a republic or a monarchy?" The argument on each side,—the riddle read.

III. Military Affairs.

1. *War with Spain* [1667–68]:—Invasion of Flanders,—seizure of Franche Comté,—Peace of Aix-la-Chapelle.

2. *War with Holland* [1672–78]:— Its commercial cause,—its religious cause. The passage of the Rhine,—deification of humbug. Revolution in Holland,—William of Orange,—cutting of the dykes. Second seizure of Franche Comté,—Peace of Nymwegen.

LOUIS XIV.
SECOND LECTURE.

1. *Absolutism in its First Phase:*—The child's copy-book in St. Petersburg,—light streaming from it over French history. Things admirable in Louis's early character.

2. *Absolutism in its Second Phase:*—Destruction of all local powers. Quotations from Louis's memoirs to show his theory,—historical sketch to show his practice. (Citations from St. Simon and Dangeau.)

3. "*Grandeur*" *in France:*—New worship,—palace-building,—flunkeyism,—high heels and periwigs. Death of Colbert,—Madame de Maintenon and the Jesuits (La Chaise and Le Tellier). Proselytism,—by discrimination,—by bribes,—by penalties,—the dragonnades. Revocation of the Edict of Nantes [1685],—its results.

4. "*Glory*" *in Europe:*—Louis's attempt to browbeat Europe,—return of English captives to the Algerines,—bombardment of Genoa,—insult to the Pope,—the Chambers of Reunion. Louis's attempt to bribe Europe. William of Orange and the League of Augsburg [1686]. The Revolution in England [1688], War of the League of Augsburg [1688–97],—burning of the Palatinate,—Peace of Ryswick [1697].

5. "*Grandeur*" *and* "*Glory*" *to be Paid for:*—Vauban's picture of French wretchedness. Progress of tyranny,—disgrace of Vauban,—of Racine,—of Fénelon,—the secret police,—*lettres de cachet*. "Glory" gives a last bright flicker. War of the Spanish Succession [1701–1714],—weakness of despotism,—Marlborough,—Peace of Utrecht [1714]. Last days of Louis,—his death [1715],—his burial. The secret of his failure.

BOSSUET AND FÉNELON.

FIRST LECTURE.

I. Bossuet.

1. *Early Years:*—His birth [1627],—his family. His precocity,—his early veneration for the Sacred Books,—he receives the tonsure at eight, and is made a canon at thirteen.

2. *His Education:*—At Dijon under the Jesuits,—at Paris under Nicolas Cornet. Influence of Cornet,—of the political life of the time,—of St. Vincent de Paul. Bossuet's early eloquence,—incident of the Hôtel de Rambouillet,—his firmness of character. He takes his doctor's degree [1652].

3. *Bossuet at Metz:*—He enters the priesthood, and is made Archdeacon of Metz. His work at Metz,—efforts against Protestantism,—difference between his personal and his official attitude. Unsuccessful attempts to induce him to return to Paris,—his sermon before the queen regent and Mazarin [1657],—its twofold result.

4. *Bossuet at Paris:*—His eloquence,—his devotion to study,—his erudition. He is made Bishop of Condom,—is admitted to the Academy. Character of his oratory,—his deference to royalty,—his funeral orations (over Queen Henrietta of England,—over the duchess of Orleans,—over the prince of Condé),—their largeness of view.

5. *Bossuet and Protestantism:*—The *Exposition de la Doctrine Catholique* [1661],—its power in statement,—its

concessions. The *Histoire des Variations des Églises Protestantes* [1688],—Bossuet and Chillingworth.

6. *Bossuet and Jansenism :*—The Port-Royalists,—contumacy of the nuns,—Bossuet's effort to convert them,—revolt of his better nature. His work on the Port-Royal translation of the Bible.

7. *Bossuet Preceptor to the Dauphin* [*1670-79*] *:*—Dignity of the office,—popularity of his appointment,—worthlessness of the royal pupil. Bossuet's devotion to his work,—his letter to the Pope,—his works for the use of the dauphin,—the *Traité de la Connaissance de Dieu et de Soi-même,*—the *Histoire Universelle,*—its importance in the history of historical writing,—Bossuet's philosophy of history,—distorting influence of his theology upon his selection and treatment of details,—real greatness of his plan,—the *Politique Sacrée,*—its absolutism,—Bossuet and Louis XIV. Incidental labors,—range of his studies with the dauphin,—reason of their uselessness, so far as the prince himself was concerned,—influence of his educational works upon the French people.

8. *Bossuet at Meaux :*—He is made Bishop of Meaux [1681],—reason why he received no higher appointment. The controversy between Louis XIV and Innocent XI,—the *Régale,*—the Assembly of 1682,—Bossuet becomes the champion of the "liberties of the Gallican church,"—the Four Articles. His work for the Church of Rome,—his conversions from Protestantism,—his prestige in Europe. Two illustrations of his method:—1. Bossuet and Richard Simon; 2. Bossuet and Fénelon.

BOSSUET AND FÉNELON.

SECOND LECTURE.

II. Fénelon.

1. *Early Years:*—His birth [1651],—his family,—his attractiveness. Early theological studies at St. Sulpice.

2. *First Labors:*—He seeks to go as a missionary to Canada,—to Greece,—successful opposition of his family,—is selected to work upon converted Protestants,—incurs the hatred of Harlay, Archbishop of Paris. His mastery of the French language,—early writings,—the *Traité de l'Éducation des Filles,*—the Criticism of Malebranche,—the *Traité du Ministère des Pasteurs,*—qualities common to these works. His mission to Poitou,—his noble stipulation,—his method and its success,—attacks of Harlay,—Fénelon accused of heresy,—of indifferentism.

3. *Fénelon Preceptor to the Younger Dauphin* [*1689-97*]*:* —Reasons of his appointment,—importance of the position,—character of the young Duke of Burgundy. Fénelon's wonderful success,—comparison of his method with that of Bossuet, in intellectual training,—in moral training. Fénelon's writings during this period,—the Fables,—their purpose,—the *Dialogues des Morts,*—their character and value,—arguments against despotism,—against anarchy,—the *Directions pour la Conscience d'un Roi,*—its plain words on the duties of kings to their subjects and to other nations,—the *Télémaque,*—ideas inculcated in it,—its anticipation of the *laissez-faire* theory of government,—its unconscious reproduction of living characters. His anonymous letter to the king,—its justification,—its contents,—its startling directness.

4. *Fénelon Archbishop of Cambrai:*—He is made Archbishop-Duke of Cambrai [1695],—reason why he was not made Archbishop of Paris,—resignation of his other preferments,—his influence upon his new province.

5. *Fénelon and Quietism:*—Rise of the Quietists,—Molinos,—main points of his doctrine,—its condemnation by the Pope,—its danger to the Church and to morality. Introduction of Quietism into France by Madame Guyon,—her character,—hostility of Harlay,—his persecution of her. Reasons why Fénelon defended Madame Guyon,—intervention of the "Eagle of Meaux,"—his attack upon Quietism,—Fénelon's refusal to sanction it,—publication of his own book, the *Maximes des Saints sur la Vie Intérieure* [1697]. Previous friendship of Bossuet and Fénelon,—beginning of the breach,—its results to Fénelon. Character of the *Maximes des Saints,*—general approval at first,—Bossuet's assault upon it,—success of his theologic intrigues,—attitude of the king,—condemnation of the book by the Sorbonne,—Fénelon's tutorship taken from him,—his banishment to his diocese,—further ill-treatment. The appeal to Rome,—sympathy of the Pope,—Bossuet's emissaries,—the Pope's fear of Louis,—threats of the latter,—Fénelon's book at last condemned by the Church [1699].

6. *Fénelon in Disgrace:*—His humble submission,—fraudulent publication of the *Télémaque,*—its misinterpretation,—culmination of the royal displeasure. Fénelon at Cambrai,—his treatment of Protestants,—his care of the sick and wounded,—his quiet patience.

7. *Last Years:*—Death of Bossuet [1705],—unworthy close of his life. Last years of Fénelon,—his unfaltering devotion to his work,—his manly death [1715],—undying enmity of Louis.

8. *Bossuet and Fénelon:*—Transitoriness of the work of Bossuet,—endurance of the work of Fénelon.

THE REGENCY AND LOUIS XV.

I. The Regency [1715-23].

1. *The Regent:*—His character,—Louis XIV's will broken,—condition of France.

2. *Foreign Difficulties:*—Alberoni and his plots,—Dubois and his counterplots.

3. *Domestic Difficulties:*—The debt,—expedients,—John Law and his scheme,—its wonderful success—and failure,—effect upon the national character. The plague at Marseilles,—Belzunce. The orgies at Paris,—the *roués*. Belzunce and Dubois rivals,—the cardinal's hat,—the statue.

II. Louis XV [1723-74].

1. *The Duke of Bourbon's Ministry [1723-26]:*—His character,—the king's marriage,—of "smart" policy in general and Bourbon's policy in particular.

2. *Cardinal Fleury's Ministry [1726-43]:*—His peace policy,—Fleury and Walpole. Jansenists and Jesuits,—the bull *Unigenitus,*—Christophe de Beaumont and the *billets de confession,*—intervention of the Parliament of Paris,—the miracles at Paris and St.-Médard. Death of Fleury.

3. *Cotillon Numéro Un [1743-45]:*—Madame de Châteauroux,—playing at soldiers,—a fright.

4. *Cotillon Numéro Deux [1745-64]:*—Madame de Pompadour,—her character,—her system,—Machault,—the *Parc aux Cerfs.* "Petticoat No. 2" Maria Theresa's "cousin,"—the Seven Years' War.

5. *Cotillon Numéro Trois* [*1764-74*]:—Madame du Barri,—her advent,—Du Barri and the Jesuits,—France shameless and hopeless. (Citations.)

III. Philosophy and Jesuitism.

Choiseul and the Philosophers *versus* Du Barri and the Jesuits,—Choiseul triumphant. Piety of Louis XV,—tricks,—Du Barri triumphant. Louis drawing near the end,—his indifference to consequences,—his loathsome death,—jubilation,—the mourners. Condition of the French nation,—whose was the blame?

FRENCH INSTITUTIONS BEFORE THE REVOLUTION.

I. The Old Triple Body of Wrong.

1. Old selfish *Laws*—fostering Inequality.
2. Old selfish *Habits*—fostering Confusion.
3. Old selfish *Men*—fostering Oppression.

II. The Church.

1. *Its Inequalities :*—Inequality in dioceses,—in revenues.

2. *Its Oppression :*—Its hatred of new thought,—its persecutions of Protestants,—the Calas and Sirven affairs,—attempts at repression of thought,—insincerity of all this.

3. *Its Corruption :*—Dubois,—Tencin and Lafitau,—spread of this internal corruption,—anecdotes.

III. The State.

1. *Royalty :*—Villeroi's speech,—"despotism tempered by epigrams,"—royal·ordinances,—*lits de justice,*—royal taxation,—*lettres de cachet,*—"Madame de Pompadour's little whims, you know." Absolutism defiant to the last,—Louis's dying confession.

2. *Nobility :*—Noblesse and Roturiers,—the gulf,—discriminations,—caste,—exemptions,—privileges. Spirit of the nobles. Their number.

3. *The Parliament of Paris :*—Its composition,—pur-

chase of judgeships,—the legal caste. Its functions,—registry,—the "bed of justice,"—harsher treatment,—weakness of the Parliament.

4. *The Assembly of Notables:*—its composition —its defects.

5. *The States-General:*—Its composition,—its uncertain character,—its long disuse.

6. *Administration:*—A. *General Administration.* The Ministers,—mixture of functions,—sale of offices,—sinecures. B. *Military Affairs.* C. *Justice.* Confusion of provincial courts and customs,—bad principles in procedure,—preliminary torture,—denial of counsel,—concealment of charges,—presumption of guilt,—barbarous modes of punishment,—case of Damiens,—of De la Barre,—the wheel. D. *Finance.* Carelessness of the state credit,—inequality in taxation,—the Farmers-General,—ignorance of political economy,—protection.

IV. The People.

Hatred created in the richer class by inequality. Misery created in the poorer class by oppression,—false ideas of labor,—feudal exactions. The French peasantry as caricatured by Gillray,—as described by Arthur Young,—Robert Miron's figure,—statistics,—a personal reminiscence. Secret of this oppression.

THE FRENCH PHILOSOPHERS OF THE XVIIIth CENTURY.

I. Their Rise.

1. *Transition* from the Classic literature of Louis XIV's time to the Philosophic literature of Louis XV's time,—Mignet's remark.

2. *First Suggestions* of reform,—alliance of the Church with despotism (Guizot's statement),—results of this alliance,—a new influence (Buckle's researches).

II. Montesquieu [1689-1755].

1. *First Period:*—His origin, — his official position. The *Lettres Persanes* [1721].

2. *Second Period:*—His travels,—visit to England. The *Causes de la Grandeur et de la Décadence des Romains* [1734],—its value,—Napoleon's opinion of it,—Buckle's opinion. The *Esprit des Lois* [1748].

III. Voltaire [1694-1778].

1. *His Early Years:*—His birth,—his name. His waywardness,—his genius,—his education by the Jesuits.

2. *His Writings:*—First writings,— tragedies,— the *Henriade*,—the *Lettres philosophiques*,—the *Essai sur les Mœurs*,—*La Pucelle*.

3. *His Life:*—His attitude toward monarchy,—his personal morality,—lack of calmness and dignity in his life. His life at Cirey,—at the court of Frederick the Great,—at Ferney. Nobler phase of his life near its close,—the

Calas affair,—its results,—Beccaria and the abolition of torture. His life as a whole,—contradictions in his character. His death,—his burial.

4. *His Influence :*—Voltaire's real conservatism,—as to politics,—as to society,—as to religion,—" tearing down."

IV. Rousseau [1712–1778].

His early life and pursuits. The two prize essays,—the *Contrat social,*—the *Profession de Foi du Vicaire savoyard.*

V. The Encyclopedists and Materialists.

1. The *Encyclopédie,*—Diderot,—D'Alembert,—Condorcet.
2. Raynal,—Helvétius,—Holbach.

VI. The Philosophic Queens and Courts.

Transfer of influence from the Court at Versailles to certain courts in Paris parlors,—Mesdames de Tencin, Geoffrin, Du Deffand, L'Espinasse, and others,—consequences.

VII. The Attack on Institutions.

1. *On the Church* [up to 1750.—*Buckle*].
2. *On the State* [after 1750.—*Buckle*].
3. *The Effect.*

THE SUPPRESSION OF THE JESUIT ORDER.

I. The Preparation.

1. Significance of this history.

2. Recapitulation of the history of the order: (*a*) In France, (*b*) in Germany, (*c*) in Spain, (*d*) in Portugal.

3. Difficulties of the Papacy with the Order.

4. Forces opposed to the Jesuits in the eighteenth century. (*a*) Strict moralists in the Church (Pascal,—Möhler's apology and statement regarding Protestantism). (*b*) Opposition of the old orders. (*c*) Opposition of sundry mercantile interests. (*d*) Opposition of the philosophers of the eighteenth century. (*e*) Feeling of certain vigorous statesmen. (*f*) Personal alarms of sundry monarchs at Jesuit casuistry.

II. The Suppression by Civil Governments.

1. Pombal's struggle in Portugal,—mixture of motives,—punishment of the Tavora family, the Jesuit Malagrida, and others,—suppression of the Order in Portugal [1759].

2. Choiseul's struggle in France,—mixture of motives,—Madame de Pompadour's grievance,—the Lavalette case,—answer to the plea of Louis XV for the Order,—its suppression in France [1764].

3. Charles III, D'Aranda, Campomanes, and the struggle in Spain,—insurrection in Madrid,—part taken by the Jesuits in calming the people,—results on the King's mind,—consequent careful preparations,—the suppression in Spain [1767],—its severity.

4. Tanucci and the suppression in Naples.

5. Similar measures in Austria under Joseph II,—also under minor princes, especially those of the House of Bourbon.

III. The Suppression by the Pope.

1. Attempts to induce the Pope to suppress the Order,—refusals of Clement XIII,—efforts after his death to elect a Pope pledged to suppression.

2. Election of Ganganelli, as Clement XIV,—his efforts to avoid the suppression,—stubbornness of Ricci ("*Sint ut sunt, aut non sint*"),—accumulated pressure, especially from Spain,—Florida Blanca and his mission.

3. Papal suppression by the brief *Dominus ac Redemptor* [1773],—imprisonment and death of Ricci,—legends as to the misery and insanity of Clement XIV and his assassination by the Jesuits,—calumnies heaped upon his memory,—Theiner's opinion.

IV. Resurrection of the Order.

1. Protection afforded to the Jesuits by Frederick the Great,—his reasons. Protection afforded by Catharine II,—her reasons. Preservation of the Order mainly in Russia.

2. Restoration of the Order by Pius VII in 1814 by the bull *Sollicitudo Omnium*,—expulsions and recalls of the Jesuits by various nations since,—their eclipse in Germany and Switzerland,—their triumph in Rome and in Belgium.

3. Their relations to modern Science (Boscowitch and Secci),—to History (Loriquet and Fredet),—to Missions (De Smet and others),—to Education. Virtues and vices of the Order,—similarity of certain developments in Protestantism,—the true solvent for "Jesuitic" efforts of every sort.

LOUIS XVI.

I. The New King and Queen.

1. *The King :*—His character as variously sketched and as it was,—his portraits,—his childhood,—his Christian spirit,—his writings,—his studies and occupations,—his bravery.

2. *The Queen :*—Her character as variously sketched and as it was,—her impulsiveness and its results,—her education,—her courage and energy.

3. *First Acts :*—The *joyeux avénement*,—recall of the Parliament,—choice of a prime minister.

4. *Maurepas :*—His character,—his policy.

II. Turgot [1774-76].

His birth and education,—early writings,—his breadth of mind,—his position as philosopher and statesman. His work at Limoges. Turgot Controller-General of Finances,—his ministry. Malesherbes. Reaction.

III. Necker [1776-81].

Action again. Character of Necker,—attempts at financial reform,—the *Compte rendu*,—failure,—dismissal.

IV. Calonne [1783-87].

His gorgeous new system of finance,—brilliancy of his financial pyrotechny,—pyrotechnics burnt out,—the Assembly of Notables.

V. Lomenie de Brienne [1787-88].

His character,—his dealings with the Notables,—his dealings with the Parliament,—his dismissal (with full pockets).

VI. " Encore du Neckerisme tout pur."

Necker recalled,—he determines to summon the States-General.

VII. The Stream of New Thought through this Age.

1. *The Main Stream.*

2. *Tributaries:*—Three tributaries from the American Republic,—tributaries from Voltaire at Paris and from Rousseau's grave,—from Necker's *Compte rendu*,—from the Clubs,—from *Figaro*,—from the Necklace affair,—from Jansenism and Calvinism,—from Science,—from Quackery.

VIII. The States-General [1789].

1. *Preliminaries:*—The two questions,—the Notables again,—the struggle,—the decision,—Siéyès's *Qu'est-ce que le Tiers État?*—the elections.

2. *The Meeting* [5 May 1789] :—1614 and 1789.

TURGOT.

1. *His Birth and Education* [*1727-1750*].—Position of Turgot in the history of France,—his greatness, even in failure. His ancestry,—his birth [1727],—ancestral and personal characteristics. His destination for the Church, —his career at Saint Sulpice,—his essay on paper money, in answer to Terrasson [1749]. His career at the Sorbonne,—his election as Prior,—his two discourses. His decision to change his career,—attempts of Brienne, Boisgelin, and other friends to dissuade him,—his answer.

2. *His Early Manhood* [*1751-1761*] :—His legal career,—his contributions to the *Encyclopédie*,—his *Lettres sur la Tolérance* [1753]. Financial administration in France since Colbert,—results of carelessness regarding the national credit. Beginnings of modern political economy,—the Economists, or Physiocrats,—Quesnay and Gournay,—their influence on Turgot, theoretically and practically.

3. *Turgot Intendant at Limoges* [*1761-1774*] :—Abolition of the *corvée* for public works and military transportation,—breaking down of barriers to internal commerce,—mitigation of suffering,—other improvements,— his success. His refusal of promotion,—his dispatches to the ministry regarding national reforms. Writings of this period,—his treatise *Sur la Formation et la Distribution des Richesses*,—its relation to Adam Smith's "Wealth of Nations",—his treatise *Sur les Prêts d'Argent*,—his letters *Sur la Liberté du Commerce des Grains*.

4. *Turgot Controller-General of the Finances* [*1774–*

1776] :—Accession of Louis XVI,—Turgot made Minister of Naval Affairs,—his promotion to the Ministry of Finance,—his proposals to the King regarding financial policy,—their accomplishment,—his advice to the King in the matter of the coronation oath. His *memorandum on the organization of municipalities*,—twofold method of education proposed. The *edict for free trade in grain*,—opposition,—insurrection,—weakness of the King,—firmness of Turgot. The *edict for the suppression of the corvée*,—bitter opposition of the Parliament of Paris,—forced registry. The *edict for the suppression of the maîtrises and jurandes*,—old system of arts and trades in France,—tyrannies, jealousies, and abuses,—legal difficulties arising out of these,—renewed opposition of the Parliament,—forced registry again. Turgot's measures regarding the *taille*,—abolition of the *contrainte solidaire*,—prevention of evasions of nobles and clergy,—his conduct towards the farmers-general,—public works.

5. *Turgot's Fall* :—Hostility of the Court and nobility, of the leaders of the Third Estate, and of the clergy,—causes of this,—secret hostility of Maurepas,—court intrigues and forged letters,—Turgot's dismissal [1776],—his retirement and death [1781].

6. *Reflections* :—Of Turgot's administration as a turning-point in French history,—importance of study upon this, and upon similar crises in the history of Great Britain and of the United States.

THE INFLUENCE OF AMERICAN IDEAS UPON THE FRENCH REVOLUTION.

FIRST LECTURE.

Purpose of this lecture,—review of the period preceding the French Revolution,—want of practical direction to French ideas of liberty and reform,—general influence of America in giving this practical direction,—special influences.

I. The Influence of Franklin.

1. On the nation directly. 2. Through Turgot. 3. Through Condórcet. 4. Through Champfort. 5. Through Moréllet. 6. Through others, of whom Mirabeau and Chénier are representatives.

II. The Influence of Jefferson.

1. Reciprocal influence between Jefferson and the leaders of French thought.

2. Jefferson's influence through Lafayette, — through Rabaut St.-Étienne, — through the Girondists, — federal ideas of the Girondists.

3. Relations with Robespierre falsely imputed to Jefferson,—the dividing line between American influence and want of influence in the French Revolution.

III. The Influence of French Officers returned from the American Revolution.

1. *Lafayette:*—His influence in bringing on the French Revolution,—in shaping it,—his draft of the Declaration of Rights.

2. *Rochambeau:*—His character,—peculiarities of his growth in Americanism.

3. *Ségur:*—Light thrown on French feeling regarding America by his memoirs,—his own impressions.

4. The French soldiery,—effect of familiarizing them with ideas of liberty and equality,—detection by Arthur Young of American ideas in the early Revolutionary ferment.

THE INFLUENCE OF AMERICAN IDEAS UPON THE FRENCH REVOLUTION.

SECOND LECTURE.

IV. The Influence of Frenchmen returned from American Travel.

1. *Chástellux:*—Difference in spirit between that and the recent race of travelers in America,—causes of Chastellux's great influence.

2. *Brissot "de Warville":*—Clavière's letter of suggestions,—Brissot's book,—Brissot the first open Republican in France.

3. *Mazzei, Crèvecœur,* and others.

V. Summary of the American Influences.

1. *Familiarity with the idea of Revolution.*

2. *Strength given to French ideas of Liberty:*—New meanings of the word Liberty,—Chénier's ode,—Fauchet's sermon,—Anacharsis Clootz's tribute.

3. *Practical shape given to ideas of Equality:*—Vagueness of these ideas previously,—remarks of Sir Henry Maine on this,—proofs from the constitutions of 1791, '93, and '95.

4. *Practical combination of Liberty and Equality into institutions*, republican and democratic. Brissot's writings,—Camille Desmoulins' *La France libre*,—indirect testimony of Portiez.

5. *An ideal of republican manhood:*—Chénier's apostrophe to Washington and Franklin. Sauvigny's tragedy of "*Vashington, ou la Liberté du Nouveau Monde,*"—ex-

tracts, to show its absurdities,—summary, to show its real significance.

6. American influence on the French Revolution a source of just pride,—that influence coördinate with the *greatness* of that Revolution,—it ceases when the Revolution degenerates.

VI. Lesson of this History for the America of To-day.

1. How this American influence on Europe was lost.
2. How alone it may be regained.

THE FRENCH REVOLUTION.

I. TO THE FORMATION OF THE NATIONAL ASSEMBLY.

1 JANUARY–17 JUNE 1789.

I. The First Step out of National Insignificance.

The Edict of the 1st of January, 1789 :—Number of deputies in each of the three orders,—effect of the edict on France,—its significance.

II. The Elections.

1. *The Election Machinery:* — Its complexity, — its leading features.
2. The *Cahiers de Doléances*.
3. *Jarring in the Machinery* :—In Brittany,—throughout France.

III. The Deputies in General.

1. *The Clergy* :—The hierarchy,—the working clergy.
2. *The Nobles.*
3. *The Third Estate:* — Burke's ravings, — Alison's twaddle,—*preponderance of lawyers*,—advantages and disadvantages of this,—distinction to be made,—De Tocqueville's remark. Burke's second objection—*want of sufficient admixture of a prosperous middle-class*,—cause of this want. Burke's third objection—*want of practical men*,—cause of this want. Taine's objections, founded and unfounded.

IV. The Leaders.

1. *Among the Clergy* :—Maury,—Talleyrand.
2. *Among the Nobility* :—The Duke of La Rochefoucauld,—Cazalès,—the Duke of Orleans,—Lafayette.

3. *Among the Third Estate:*—Mirabeau,—Sieyès,—Robespierre.

V. The Cahiers de Doléances.

1. Demands of the Clergy.   2. Demands of the Nobility.   3. Demands of the Third Estate.

VI. Opening of the States-General.

1. *Religious Ceremonies* [*4 May 1789*] :—The procession,—sermon of the Bishop of Nancy.

2. *The First Session* [*5 May*] :—The *Salle des Menus*,—de Brézé and etiquette,—speech of the King,—of Barentin,—of Necker.

3. *The Second Session* [*6 May*] :—The Third Estate meets alone, but in the great hall,—importance of the latter fact.

4. *The Unsettled Question :*—Shall the States-General be a consolidated assembly or an assembly of three distinct orders?—greatness of the question,—calmness and statesmanship of the Third Estate,—their courage and determination,—conferences,—the appeal to the Clergy [27 May],—Sieyès's great motion,—the deputies of the Third Estate become the NATIONAL ASSEMBLY [17 June 1789].

THE FRENCH REVOLUTION.

II. FROM THE FORMATION OF THE NATIONAL ASSEMBLY TO THE STORMING OF THE BASTILLE.

17 JUNE–14 JULY 1789.

I. Attempts of the Court to Outwit the Assembly.

1. *Anger of the Court Party* at the declaration of the 17th of June,—the Clergy vote to unite with the Commons,—obstinacy of the Noblesse,—Necker's attempt at compromise,—project of a Royal Sitting.

2. *Exclusion of the Assembly* from their hall,—oath of the *Jeu de Paume,* or *Tennis-court Oath* [20 June 1789].

3. *New Annoyances,*—the session in the Church of St. Louis,—the majority of the Clergy join the National Assembly.

II. Attempts to Overawe the Assembly.

1. *The Royal Sitting* [23 June]:—Etiquette and indignities,—the King's speech,—annulment of the Assembly's decrees,—the Assembly commanded to disperse,—departure of the King, with the Clergy and Nobles.

2. *Who is Supreme?*—Mirabeau and Brézé,—the Assembly openly disobeys the King,—the declaration of inviolability,—the Assembly goes on with its work.

3. *Victory of the Third Estate:*—Return of the Clergy,—secession of a part of the Nobility,—final fusion of the three orders [27 June].

III. Attempts to Coerce the Assembly.

1 *Concentration of troops,* — ominous bearing of the Nobles,—feeling of the French people,—petition of the Assembly.

2. *Dismissal of Necker* [11 July],—the new ministry,—Breteuil and Broglie,—the plot develops,—preparations for action.

IV. Beginning of Open Revolution at Paris.

1. The *Palais Royal*,—why it became a centre of insurrection.

2. Camille Desmoulins and the uprising of Paris [12 July],—the committee of electors,—organization of the National Guard.

THE FRENCH REVOLUTION.

III. FROM THE STORMING OF THE BASTILLE TO THE ABOLITION OF FEUDAL PRIVILEGE.

14 JULY–4 AUGUST 1789.

I. The Bastille Conquest.

1. *The Bastille:*—Its history,—its construction,—its government,—its relations to French society.

2. *The Fourteenth of July:*—Arming of the people,—resolution of all popular cries into the cry against the Bastille.

3. *Cause of this popular hatred* against a *prison for nobles*,—Louis Blanc's explanation,—the true explanation,—the Bastille an outward and visible sign of inward political evil.

4. *The Attack:*—The Faubourg Saint-Antoine,—parleying and fighting,—the weapons, and the spirit in which the people used them.

5. *The Surrender,*—the "Bastille unveiled,"—release of the prisoners.

II. The First Ferocities.

1. Violation of the capitulation,—murder of Delaunay and a part of the garrison.

2. Murder of Flesselles.

III. Philosophy of French Revolutionary Ferocity.

1. Possibility of a national training to cruelty or humanity,—examples.

2. *First Agency in the Education of the French Nation to Cruelty:*—Certain ideas fostered in the Church.

3. *Second Agency :*—Certain institutions cherished in the State.

4. *Third Agency :*—Long-continued oppression and ignorance.

5. How this ferocity might have been checked,—lesson for our own country.

IV. Effects of the Bastille Conquest.

1. *On the Assembly and the King :*—Concessions of the latter,—Bailly, Lafayette, and the new municipality,—the King's visit to Paris.

2. *On the People :*—In the provinces,—destruction of castles and title-deeds. At Paris,—murder of Foulon and Berthier.

3. *On the Nobles :*—The "Emigration",—the sacrifices of the night of the Fourth of August.

THE FRENCH REVOLUTION.
IV. FROM THE ABOLITION OF FEUDAL PRIVILEGE TO THE REMOVAL OF THE KING TO PARIS.
4 AUGUST–6 OCTOBER 1789.

I. Real Nature of the Concessions of the Fourth of August.

1. As shown by the general history of privileged classes.
2. As shown by sundry special histories.
3. As shown by Louis XVI's letter to the Archbishop of Arles.
4. As shown by the debates on making these concessions laws.

II. The Declaration of Rights.

1. Main things said for and against such declarations.
2. How the French Declaration differed from the English Bill of Rights.
3. Variety and ability of the projects presented to the Assembly.
4. Vicious methods of debating.
5. The Declaration of Rights as adopted.

III. First Work on the Constitution.

1. The two great parties,—sources of their ideas.
2. The question of the *duration of the national legislature.*
3. The question of a *single or double assembly.*
4. The question of the *royal sanction*—the *veto.*

IV. Four New Portents.

1. *Anarchy:*—Exhibitions of this in the capital and in the provinces.

2. *Famine:*— Suffering, — selfishness, — mob superstitions,—ferocity.

3. *Threatened Bankruptcy:*—Failure of government resources and credit,—stolidity of the Assembly,—Mirabeau rescues Necker.

4. *Wild Journalism:*—Camille Desmoulins and the *Révolutions de France et de Brabant,*—Peltier and the *Actes des Apôtres,*—Loustalot and the *Révolutions de Paris,* —Marat and the *Ami du Peuple,*—Hébert and the *Père Duchêne.*

V. A New Plot and its Results.

1. Court life in this emergency,—new plot by Court and Nobles,—attitude of the King,—more troops.

2. Banquet of the body guard at Versailles [2 Oct.],— the orgies.

3. *Insurrection of the Fifth and Sixth of October:*— The "Insurrection of Women",—march of the mob on Versailles,—the King brought to Paris.

4. The plot foiled,—secret of it,—its moral.

THE FRENCH REVOLUTION.

V. FROM THE REMOVAL OF THE KING TO PARIS TO THE FEDERATION FESTIVAL.

6 OCTOBER 1789–14 JULY 1790.

I. Background of the Assembly Picture.

The popular ferment,—Marat,—the *Ça Ira*,—Camille Desmoulins as "*Procureur-Général de la Lanterne.*" Sufferings of the people,—tendencies shown in the François murder. The Assembly's provision for martial law,—the Municipality's "search committee,"—importance of this.

II. The New Monarchy.

1. *Change in the monarchical theory*,—the King a Chief Magistrate.
2. *Consequences* flowing from this as to legislation,—as to taxation,—as to decision regarding war and peace.

III. The New Administrative System.

1. The old Provinces,—evils inseparable from their origin.
2. The new Departments,—Districts,—Communes.
3. Abolition of interior frontiers,—avoidance of a federative system.

IV. The New Electoral System.

1. Electoral divisions,—the Canton.
2. Attempt to co-ordinate right and security,—active and passive citizens.
3. Final abolition of voting by orders.

4. Abolition of religious disabilities, Protestant and Jewish.

5. Compromise theory of representation adopted.

V. The New System of Criminal Procedure.

1. Abolition of *lettres de cachet*,—of secrecy,—of torture,—of attainder and confiscation,—of privileged classes of criminals,—of carelessness in capital cases.

2. Robespierre attempts to abolish capital punishment,—Guillotin and the guillotine.

3. Establishment of approved safeguards in criminal cases,—the jury.

VI. The New Organization of the Judiciary.

1. Abolition of the old Parliaments and of the "venal system,"—indemnities to former judges.

2. Establishment of an elective judiciary,—its advantages,—its one vast disadvantage.

VII. The State Church System.

1. Appropriation of the property of the Church.

2. Suppression of monastic orders,—Garat's argument,—indemnities to monks and others,—lesson from this.

3. Civil constitution of the clergy.

VIII. The New Financial System.

The *Assignats*,—their use, in theory and in practice. The report of Camus, and publication of the *Livre rouge*.

IX. The Federation Festival.

First anniversary of the fall of the Bastille,—preparation of the *Champ de Mars*,—Paris at work,—the federation ceremonies [14 July 1790],—their significance.

Court of appeal
Crim. court – with jury
Civil court – no jury.
District court – police judge, or perhaps just. of p.
Court to settle quarrels of family.
Commercial courts.

'85. To meet deficit, [illegible] taxes, 12,500,000 f
& this not enough. So [illegible] eyes turn
church, wh. owned 1/3 of landed property, [illegible]
illions of francs. [illegible] used in luxury
debauching men. Tithes abolished. [illegible]
blic ready for more. Talleyrand came
rward; said church held it in trust f
ation, and nation might therefore [illegible]
provided ~~the~~ nation would take care of
urch. Mirabeau said, [illegible] [illegible]
[illegible] and take [illegible]. Give pensions [illegible]
[illegible] they've never had, [illegible] [illegible].

[illegible] said civil suicide [illegible] [illegible]

It is nf. from a [illegible] elect
[illegible] by [illegible]-court o[illegible]
[illegible] con[illegible] [illegible]
1[?]-1787
[illegible]

THE FRENCH REVOLUTION.

VI. FROM THE FEDERATION FESTIVAL TO THE CLOSE OF THE NATIONAL ASSEMBLY.

14 JULY 1790–30 SEPTEMBER 1791.

I. The Clubs.

1. *The Jacobins:*—Origin of the club,—its name,—its membership,—its organization,—its growth,—its objects.

2. *The Cordeliers:*—Reason of their secession from the Jacobins.

3. *The Feuillants:*—Lafayette,—why the club failed.

II. The Main Series of Internal Difficulties and Dangers.

1. *Clash between liberty and discipline* in the army,—Bouillé at Nancy [Aug. 1790].

2. *The new financial difficulties,*—flight of Necker [Sept. 1790].

3. *The Clergy refractory.*

4. *The Nobility refractory.*

5. *Death of Mirabeau* [2 April 1791].

6. *Flight of the King* [20 June 1791],—his arrest at Varennes,—consequences.

7. *Affray of the Field of Mars.*

III. The Main Series of External Difficulties and Dangers.

1. *The Emigration,*—character and plots of the *emigres*.

2. *Coalition of foreign powers,*—the Conference of Mantua,—the Declaration of Pilnitz [27 Aug. 1791].

3. *Conduct of England,*—light thrown upon this by her more recent conduct towards our own country.

IV. Summary of the Work done by the National Assembly.

1. *In Asserting and Daring.*.
2. *In Destroying.*
3. *In Building,*—constitutions which have grown and constitutions which have been built.
4. The self-denying ordinance.
5. Close of the National Constituent Assembly [30 Sept. 1791].

tional assembly, or convention — This of the
is a legislature, and reject [illegible]
[illegible] — [illegible] the receipts,
[illegible] — It is
proposed [illegible] that excluded members
[illegible], all [illegible] of [illegible] and
— People hit [illegible] for [illegible] party to
next election. — Right wanted to [illegible]
constitution, Supported by Lafayette and
[illegible]. Centre inclined to right. No pure
[illegible] centre as in former assembly.
[illegible] from Gironde District near Bordeaux, &
F——, Mme Roland and Sieyès [illegible]
[illegible] — Mounier [illegible] [illegible] at [illegible]
Const. brought — at opening session, and
over allegiance.— New messenger is [illegible]
[illegible]. He refuses to receive [illegible], and [illegible]
will come in a few days. Reprisals —
[illegible] duties of [illegible] and Mess[illegible], and
a close [illegible] [illegible] [illegible] [illegible] —
[illegible] Rescind this. [illegible] is [illegible] [illegible]
[illegible] to [illegible] by [illegible] [illegible] [illegible]
[illegible], [illegible] it often [illegible], [illegible]
first amnesty from the Left right
[illegible] [illegible] and then [illegible] [illegible] at

THE FRENCH REVOLUTION.

VII. FROM THE OPENING OF THE NATIONAL LEGISLATIVE ASSEMBLY TO THE BREAKING OUT OF THE WAR WITH EUROPE.

1 OCTOBER 1791–20 APRIL 1792.

I. The Legislative Assembly.

1. Its relation to other assemblies during the Revolution.

2. Its general character,—results of Robespierre's self-denying ordinance,—lassitude of the people,—unwieldiness of the Assembly.

II. Parties in the Assembly.

1. The Right, or Conservative party (Feuillants),—Ramond, Vaublanc, Dumas.

2. The Centre, or Moderate party.

3. The Left, or Radical party,—the Girondist,—Brissot, Vergniaud, Condorcet.

4. The germ of an Ultra Revolutionary party ("the Mountain"),—Chabot, Bazire, Meriin, Carnot.

III. The Opening Sessions.

1. Ceremonies,—the oaths,—the "theatrical" element in the French Revolution.

2. The new court masterpiece,—reprisals.

3. Reconciliation between King and Assembly,—impossibility of its permanence.

IV. Further Development of Opposition to Liberty.

1. The King's brother and the other Emigrants.

2. The refractory priests.

V. Efforts against this Opposition Foiled by King and Court.
  1. Law against the King's brother,—his defiant parody.
  2. Law against the Emigrants,—the King vetoes it.
  3. Law against the refractory priests,—the King vetoes it.
  4. The King's prejudice against the constitutional clergy.
  5. Court manœuvres,—the cage caricature,—Lafayette and Pétion in the mayoralty contest,—defeat of the former by the Court.

VI. Confusion.
  1. The massacres of Avignon.
  2. The massacres of St. Domingo.

to them was damned

T. Law passed that King's brother is no right to regency at King's death unless he retd in 3(?) mobuths. — Emp [...] lat did not return to be guilty of treas [...]ath and confiscation, except as rega[...] loyal heirs. — Priests to be deprived o [...]alary, house, pension; if guilty of sedit[...] [...] or imprisoned. — K[...] urged to tak [...] court priest for confessor. He refuse and stood firm on ground that con[...] granted right of conscience

Daughter of Marie Antoinette [...] married declared barred of [...] [...] priest who took of [...]

Avignon annexed to France — [...] [...]ties. French [...] into [...]

... from Tangier ... was ...
... of ... peace policy
France ...
... ... take ... — of
... applied ...
... old system. ... said, France
... and then proposed to ...
... arms. ... was ... from
... side.

III. — 2. Two divisions ... at ...
... Bull Run.

III. Mall... ... sent to ...
... of troops against ...
... grants. All ... ...
... had no ... — the ...

2. Read ... was ...
... unpleasant advice. Assembly ...
+ the reports of ... ...
Grandpost ... ...

THE FRENCH REVOLUTION.

VIII. FROM THE BREAKING OUT OF THE WAR WITH EUROPE TO THE INSURRECTION OF THE TENTH OF AUGUST.

20 APRIL–10 AUGUST 1792.

I. War with Europe Drawing On.

1. Warlike attitude of the Continent.

2. The Gironde forces the King into an attitude of war,—the Girondists taken into the ministry,—Roland and Dumouriez.

3. Opposition of Robespierre to the war,—motives assigned him by Quinet, Von Sybel, and others,—the probable truth.

4. Ultimatum of France to Austria,—ultimatum of Austria to France,—comparative responsibility of France and Austria for the great war now begun.

II. War Declared.

1. The declaration of war [20 April 1792],—disposition of the French forces.

2. Disaster of the French in Belgium,—naturalness of panics at such times.

3. Firmness of the Assembly,—decree for permanent session,—against the refractory priests,—for a camp of twenty thousand men near Paris.

III. The King still Opposes the Nation.

1. Bertrand de Moleville's *Claque* scheme,—Chambonne's corruption scheme,—Mallet du Pan's secret mission.

2. Roland's letter,—dismissal of the Girondist ministers.

3. Veto of the decree for the camp,—indignation of Paris.

4. *Insurrection of the Faubourgs* [20 June 1792],—invasion of the Tuileries,—courage and firmness of the King,—violation of the legislative body,—importance of this.

5. Temporary and ineffectual reaction.

6. Bourrienne's reminiscence of this Twentieth of June,—significance of Napoleon's remark, in view of later French history.

IV. The First European Coalition against the Revolution.

1. Attitude of England,—Priestley and Price.

2. Manifesto of the King of Prussia,—what it revealed.

3. Popular excitement in France,—Lafayette's attempt to restrain it.

4. The declaration *La patrie est en danger*,—volunteers.

5. Effect of the coalition in undermining French royalty.

V. War of the Coalition.

1. The Duke of Brunswick,—his plan,—his manifesto [25 July 1792].

2. Effect of the manifesto,—attacks upon royalty,—Brissot and Pétion,—feeling in the provinces.

3. More assignats,—the insurrectionary committee,—assassination.

4. Results of the old Court hatred for Lafayette.

into legislature. No vated resistance to [?] under Mirabeau. The [cant?] transfer of authority under forts. It happen thus [both?]

Napoleon said, "[shoot down the first?] [?] [?] and the rest will [believe?]

V. England most [powerful?], a coalition [?] [?] [?] [?] [?] [?] [?] [?] to consist [?]

2. Russia's [excuse?]: [?] [?] [?] [?]

3. Lafayette appeared in Paris at the [?] for leaders & most of [?]

4. Dramatic [dedum?]. — [?] [?] [?] [?] great influence on such action as the French. Volunteers came

THE FRENCH REVOLUTION.

IX. FROM THE INSURRECTION OF THE TENTH OF AUGUST TO THE CLOSE OF THE NATIONAL LEGISLATIVE ASSEMBLY.

10 AUGUST–21 SEPTEMBER 1792.

I. Insurrection of the Tenth of August.

1. Its beginnings,—preparations for the defense of the Tuileries,—assault of the mob,—the King takes refuge in the Assembly,—massacre of the Swiss guards.

2. Incidents,—mingled drollery, ferocity, and magnanimity.

3. Invasion of the Assembly by the mob,—deposition and confinement of the King,—abolition of the constitution of 1791,—formation of an executive council,—calling of a National Convention.

4. Santerre appointed Lafayette's successor in the command of the National Guard,—the King insulted and imprisoned in the Temple.

II. Results of the Tenth of August.

1. Increased power of the Commune and Sections of Paris.

2. Wild legislation,—regarding marriage,—regarding the unpatriotic press,—regarding property and personal liberty.

3. Anarchy,—lenity toward crime,—dealings with the murderers of Avignon and Étampes, with the shop plunderers, and with the revolted soldiers of Nanci,—Pétion's reply to the Feuillants.

4. Sales of the property of emigrants,—beginning of the great class of small proprietors.

5. Creation of a special criminal tribunal,—its lessons.

6. Differing opinions of historians as to the causes of this degeneration of the Revolution,—the main cause.

III. New Difficulties and Dangers.

1. Lafayette's despair,—his flight from France.

2. Insurrection in La Vendée.

3. Longwy taken by the Austrians,—Verdun by the Prussians,—the advance toward Paris,—condition of the French army.

IV. Desperate Measures.

1. Executions,—the decree against Longwy.

2. Danton,—domiciliary visits,—filling of the extemporized prisons. Trepidation,—the two questions,—Danton's doctrine of terrorism.

3. The September massacres [2–6 Sept. 1792]. Question as to their real authors,—the proof. Provincial imitation of these atrocities.

4. Social life of the Terrorists and of Paris at this period.

V. Victory.

1. The battle of Valmy [20 Sept. 1792],—retreat of the invaders.

2. Dissolution of the Legislative Assembly [21 Sept.],—its work. Opening of the National Convention.

THE FRENCH REVOLUTION.

X. FROM THE BEGINNING OF THE NATIONAL CONVENTION TO THE EXECUTION OF THE GIRONDISTS.

21 SEPTEMBER 1792-31 OCTOBER 1793.

FIRST LECTURE.

I. The Convention.

1. *The elections,*—influence upon them of terrorism in the cities.
2. *Character of the Convention.* Parties:—1. The Mountain,—Robespierre, Danton, Desmoulins, Marat; 2. The Gironde; 3. The Duke of Orleans and his clique; 4. The Plain, or *Marais,*—Sieyès, Cambacérès, Barère.
3. *Effect of the Argonne campaign* and the battle of Valmy,—retreat of the Prussians and Austrians,—French victories,—the Marseillaise,—Jemappes.

II. Its First Measures.

1. *Proclamation of the Republic,*—beginning of the new Republican Era [22 Sept. 1792].
2. *Beginning of the Struggle between the Mountain and the Gironde.* Rival bids for popularity,—three typical examples. Charges and counter-charges,—"*Septembriseurs*" and "*Fédéralistes*",—Louvet and Robespierre,—failure of the Girondist attack on Marat,—Girondist decree against the "*Septembriseurs*",—it is thwarted by the Mountain,—steady tendency of this wrangle.
3. *Trial and Execution of the King* [11 Dec. 1792–21 Jan. 1793]:—Jacobin pressure,—Girondist acquiescence,—noble resistance of Lanjuinais. Gamain, the iron chest, and Mirabeau. Demand of Robespierre and the

Jacobins. The King brought to trial [11 Dec.],—his counsel — (Malesherbes, Tronchet, Desèze), — charges against him,—his plan of defense,—"Louis Capet",—the three questions. Louis condemned to death,—his execution [21 Jan.],—his testament.

III. The Crisis.

1. *Effects of the King's Execution on Europe and on France:*—(a) Transfer of monarchical authority from the interior to the exterior of France. (b) Discouragement of moderate men. (c) The European coalition strengthened and stimulated to action. (d) Alarm and indifference of the people, as shown at the municipal elections. (e) Increase of crusading fanaticism in La Vendée.

2. Assassination of Lepelletier,—its results.

3. Treason of Dumouriez [April 1793], and its effect upon Girondist fortunes,—first appearance of Louis Philippe.

4. The Vendean insurrection,—revolt of Lyons,—of Corsica,—of St. Domingo,—seizure of these islands by the English.

5. Last struggle of the Girondists,—their own weapons used against them,—the Convention besieged by the mob,—proscription of the thirty-two [2 June 1793].

6. Attack, open and secret, by England,—forgery of assignats.

7. Assassination of Marat by Charlotte Corday [13 July 1793],—his deification.

8. Betrayal of Toulon to the English,—loss of fortresses and colonies,—scarcity and impending famine.

THE FRENCH REVOLUTION.

X. FROM THE BEGINNING OF THE NATIONAL CONVENTION TO THE EXECUTION OF THE GIRONDISTS.

21 SEPTEMBER 1792–31 OCTOBER 1793.

SECOND LECTURE.

IV. Jacobinism Supreme.

1. Its results abroad.
2. Its results at home.

V. Revolutionary Vigor.

1. Declaration of war against England and Holland,—new levy of troops.

2. Creation of the Revolutionary Tribunal,—its character and purpose.

3. Creation of the Committee of Public Salvation *(Salut Public)*,—its powers,—Robespierre, Couthon, and St. Just,—Cambon,—Carnot,—the Committee of General Security *(Sureté Générale)*.

4. Harsh legislation,—against the Emigrants,—against monopolies,—against royalists. *Ex post facto* laws,—requisitions,—forced loans. The *maximum*.

5. The *levée en masse*,—summary treatment of unsuccessful generals,—results.

6. The ambulatory revolutionary army and the *loi des suspects*,—certificates of civism.

7. Punishment of Lyons,—the decree,—its execution by Collot d'Herbois and Fouché. Recent parallels.

8. The Constitution of 1793,—Condorcet and Hérault-Séchelles. Its main features,—the declaration of rights,

—the executive,—the legislative,—want of checks upon popular tyranny. Its immediate suspension.

9. Abolition of titles,—"Monsieur" becomes "Citizen."

10. The new calendar,—months and *sans-culottides,*—the new names *(Vendémiaire, Brumaire, Frimaire,—Nivôse, Pluviôse, Ventôse,— Germinal, Floréal, Prairial,—Messidor, Thermidor, Fructidor)* and Carlyle's translation of them,—decimal division of month, day, and hour,—new names for holidays. Duration of the republican calendar.

11. Trial and execution of Marie Antoinette [16 Oct.], —indignities put upon her,—her noble bearing.

12. Trial and execution of the imprisoned Girondists [31 Oct.],—the main charge against them,—the gag law. Fate of the remaining Girondists,—of Roland,—of Guadet and Barbaroux,—of Pétion and Buzot,—of Condorcet. Escape of Lanjuinais and Louvet. Character of the Girondists,—causes of their downfall,—theory of Michelet,—of Louis Blanc,—of Thiers,—of Carlyle,—of Quinet,—of Lanfrey,—discussion of these.

THE FRENCH REVOLUTION.

XI. FROM THE EXECUTION OF THE GIRONDISTS TO THE DOWNFALL OF ROBESPIERRE.

31 OCTOBER 1793-27 JULY 1794.

FIRST LECTURE.

I. The Reign of Terror at Paris.

1. Exultation of the Mountain over its triumph,—medals and executions.

2. Death of Madame Roland,—of Lavoisier,—of Bailly, —of the Duke of Orleans,—of Malesherbes,—of André Chénier.

3. The Revolutionary Tribunal and its methods. Examples of denunciations, accusations, and justifications,— lists of the condemned,—devices of citizens for self-protection. Character of the public accuser (Fouquier-Tinville),—of the judges and jurors. Haste and utter recklessness of the procedure,—curious instances of this,—division of the tribunal,—steady increase in cruelty and carelessness,—case of Froidure.

4. Life in the prisons,—varying degrees of severity,— the Conciergerie.

5. Every-day life in Paris during the Reign of Terror, —recklessness and extravagance,—fashion,—gayety.

II. The Reign of Terror in the Country.

Barras at Toulon and Marseilles,—Lebon at Arras,— Maignet at Orange,—Collot d'Herbois at Lyons,—Carrier at Nantes. Fusillades and Noyades. Popular fury at St. Denis.

III. Military Energy.

1. Rising of the Republic against foreign and domestic foes.
2. Recapture of Toulon,—Bonaparte.
3. Victory at Savenay over the Vendeans.
4. Victories at Wattignies and elsewhere over the allies,—Pichegru, Hoche, Jourdan, Jourdan.

IV. Administrative Energy.

1. Need of extraordinary sources of revenue, — increased issue of paper-money,—history of this revolutionary inflation of the currency,—its results.
2. Measures to keep down prices,—the *maximum*,—its results.
3. Excellent basis of the paper currency of France,—its steady decline in spite of this,—measures to uphold it,—their futility.
4. Increasing scarcity, — tickets of subsistence, — the queues.

THE FRENCH REVOLUTION.

XI. FROM THE EXECUTION OF THE GIRONDISTS TO THE DOWNFALL OF ROBESPIERRE.

31 OCTOBER 1793–27 JULY 1794.

SECOND LECTURE.

V. Extreme Point Touched by the Revolution.

1. Evolution of new parties after the fall of the Girondists (*a.* The Robespierrists; *b.* The Dantonists, or Moderatists; *c.* The Hébertists, or Anarchists),—character of the leading men in each,—aims of each. Feeling of Robespierre toward the Dantonists and Hébertists,—the attack on religion by the Hébertists,—the renunciation of the Archbishop of Paris,—deification of Reason.

2. Feeling of the Dantonists and Hébertists toward each other,—attack of Camille Desmoulins in the *Vieux Cordelier*,—counter-attacks of Hébert. Robespierre's waiting policy,—the onslaught upon the Hébertists,—their destruction,—the onslaught upon the Dantonists,—their destruction.

VI. Beginning of Robespierre's Final Triumph.

1. The Convention decrees the existence of the Supreme Being and the immortality of the soul [7 May 1795],—continuation of judicial murders,—festival of the Supreme Being,—beginnings of an opposition party,—Jacobin dread of Robespierre as a possible tyrant,—significant concluding words of Robespierre's speech at the festival.

2. The law of the 22d Prairial (10 June),—sweeping away of all safeguards,—futile attempts against it,—its passage.

VII. Culmination of Robespierre's Final Triumph.

1. The numbers in the prisons,—size and success of the French armies,—the new Republican generals, Moreau, Pichegru, Jourdan, and others.

2. Mutual suspicion between Robespierre and many of his former adherents,—diminished number of the Convention,—precautions taken by many members against seizure,—mining and counterming,—efforts of Robespierre's enemies,—use against him of his part in the "Supreme Being" ceremonies,—Catherine Thérot. Similar feelings and efforts by Robespierre,—his avoidance of the Convention,—his working upon the Jacobins.

3. Development of the party opposed to Robespierre,—main characteristics of the leaders, Billaud-Varennes, Tallien, Barère. Robespierre's efforts to undermine them,—quotations from reports of his personal spies in the *Papiers Inédits*.

4. Rapidity of the guillotine at this crisis,—reasons of each party for letting the Terror go on.

VIII. The Ninth Thermidor.

Beginning of the struggle on the 8th Thermidor,—Robespierre's speech,—debate as to whether it should be printed and circulated. The final struggle of the 9th Thermidor (27 July 1794),—stealthy efforts of Robespierre's enemies,—the battle in the Convention,—Robespierre's defeat. Desperate efforts of his friends outside the Convention to save him,—their temporary success,—their final failure,—last hours of Robespierre and his associates,—their execution.

THE FRENCH REVOLUTION.

XII. FROM THE DOWNFALL OF ROBESPIERRE TO THE DIRECTORY.

27 JULY 1794-27 OCTOBER 1795.

FIRST LECTURE.

Resumé of the direct causes of the fall of the triumvirate,—mixture of motives.

I. The Political Reaction.

The two new parties. 1. The Thermidorians,—their main supporters and strongholds. 2. The Mountain party,—their losses in position and men,—lament of Billaud-Varennes in exile,—gradual supplanting of Terrorist members of the Committees,—decay of their influence,—attacks upon them.

II. The Social Reaction.

1. Ideas of social regeneration in the early stages of the Revolution,—Spartan and Roman ideals.

2. Reaction against these, — luxury, — effeminacy, — stock-jobbing.

3. Embodiment of this reaction in the *Jeunesse dorée* and in the *Muscadins*,—part taken in politics by these.

III. The Political Reaction becomes a Torrent.

1. Weakening and final abrogation of the *Revolutionary Tribunal,*—of the *Committees,*—of the *Jacobin Club,* —of the *Commune,*—of the *Sections.*

2. Recall of the Girondists,—restoration of confiscated property.

3. Condemnation of Carrier,—transportation of Billaud-Varennes, Collot d'Herbois, and others,—execution of Fouquier-Tinville and his associates,—the "White Terror."

IV. Increasing Misery.

1. Scarcity and suffering,—the *maximum* and its abolition.

2. Depreciation of the paper money,—Puisaye's counterfeit assignats.

V. Revolt of the Extreme Republicans.

1. Bitterness of strong republicans at the reaction,—personal misgivings of republican leaders,—popular bitterness at the general misery.

2. Attempted insurrection of the 12th Germinal.

3. *The great Insurrection of the 1st Prairial* [20 May 1795]:—Storming of the Convention,—murder of Féraud,—firmness of Boissy d'Anglas,—crushing of this insurrection.

4. Disarming of the Faubourgs.

5. Sketch of the revolutionary suburbs, and account of recent dealings with them—especially by Napoleon III.

THE FRENCH REVOLUTION.

XII. FROM THE DOWNFALL OF ROBESPIERRE TO THE DIRECTORY.

27 JULY 1794–27 OCTOBER 1795.

SECOND LECTURE.

VI. The Constitution of 1795.

1. Separation of powers takes the place of concentration of powers,—general differences between the constitutions of 1795 and 1793.

2. Citizenship,—the legislative body,—the executive body,—the declaration of duties.

3. The "Law of the Two-Thirds."

VII. Revolt of the Extreme Reactionists.

1. Vexation of the Reactionists at the Law of the Two-Thirds,—their conspiracy.

2. *Insurrection of the 13th Vendémiaire* [5 Oct. 1795], —Barras,—Bonaparte,—the Convention saved.

VIII. The Wars of the Convention.

1. New popular spirit in which these wars were carried on by France,—two causes of this. The new race of soldiers,—the new brood of generals,—the central administration,—Carnot.

2. The war against Europe,—statistics,—record of a few weeks from Montgaillard,—record of a few days from the *Moniteur*.

3. The war in the interior,—La Vendée and Brittany, —Hoche.

4. Treaties of peace,—with Tuscany and Spain,—with Prussia (Treaty of Basle, 5 April 1795).

IX. Creation of Great Institutions by the Convention.

1. The *École Normale*,—the *École Polytechnique*,—the *Lycées* and primary schools,—the *Conservatoire des Arts et Métiers*,—the national colleges of Agriculture, of Veterinary Surgery, of Oriental Languages, of Modern Languages,—the Conservatory of Music.

2. The decimal system of weights and measures.

3. The great French civil code.

4. The Institute.

X. Summary and Judgment.

1. Of various judgments on the Convention and its work.

2. Of certain plain lessons taught by its history.

THE DIRECTORY.

OCTOBER 1795–NOVEMBER 1799.

I. FROM ITS ESTABLISHMENT TO THE TREATY OF CAMPO FORMIO.

27 OCTOBER 1795–17 OCTOBER 1797.

I. The New Government.

1. Recapitulation of the constitution of 1795.
2. Character of the Directors,—Carnot and Barras,—La Reveillère-Lepaux,—Rewbell and Letourneur.

II. Difficulties of the New Government.

1. *Financial Distress:*—Assignats,—mandats,—the *tiers consolidé*,—results of all this.
2. *Popular Demoralization:*—Morality and religion,—the Theophilanthropists,—causes of their failure.
3. *Plots of the Ultra Republicans:*—Efforts of the remnant of the Jacobins,—"Communist" clubs and phrases,—Gracchus Babœuf and his armed insurrection.
4. *Plots of the Ultra Monarchists:*—Strength given them by reaction,—Augereau's *coup d'état* of the 18th Fructidor [4 Sept. 1797].

III. Military Affairs.

1. *Internal Condition:*—La Vendée and Brittany,—Hoche's "pacification."
2. *External Condition:*—Stagnation in operations against Europe,—commands assigned to Moreau, Jourdan, and Bonaparte.

IV. Bonaparte.

Early life,—education,—ideas,—first *coup d'état*,—political affiliations,—military progress.

V. The War in Italy.

1. Bonaparte's proclamation [April 1796],—Lanfrey's judgment on it,—change in the whole spirit of the war of the French Republic against Europe.

2. His campaigns against Beaulieu,—against Wurmser,—against Alvinzi,—against the Archduke Charles. Leading peculiarities of his military method.

3. His diplomacy,—two examples of its worst phases,—his dealings with Italian republicanism.

VI. The Treaty of Campo Formio.

The treaty [17 Oct. 1797],—reasons for it,—its main provisions,—different judgments of it,—its results to each of the contending powers.

THE DIRECTORY.

OCTOBER 1795-NOVEMBER 1799.

II. FROM THE TREATY OF CAMPO FORMIO TO THE EIGHTEENTH BRUMAIRE.

17 OCTOBER 1797–9 NOVEMBER 1799.

I. The Egyptian Expedition.

1. Bonaparte at Paris after his Italian campaign,—motives of Bonaparte and the Directory for bringing on the war in Egypt,—breaking with the traditional policy of France.

2. The expedition,—the voyage [May 1798]. Military successes,—moral disasters,—English attacks,—intercepted letters,—(Gillray's caricatures).

3. The Syrian campaign,—revelations of Bonaparte's untruthfulness,—Emerson's remark.

II. The War in Europe.

1. Feeling of England.
2. French war with Switzerland.
3. Congress of Rastadt and the outrage on France that ended it,—English Tory view of that crime.

III. The Return of Bonaparte to France.

1. Increasing difficulties of France,—military reverses,—Masséna at Zurich,—quarrels among the Directors.—plots and counterplots.

2. Greatness and meanness of Bonaparte shown in his return from Egypt [August 1799],—his conduct,—his tone.

IV. The Coup d'État of the Eighteenth Brumaire.

1. Position of Bonaparte and the nation.

2. Sieyès and Bonaparte conspire, — recapitulation of Sieyès's history.

3. *The Eighteenth Brumaire* [9 November 1799] :— The Directory extinguished,—the legislative bodies transferred to St. Cloud,—Bonaparte appeals to the soldiery, —final suppression of legislative authority by arms,—establishment of a provisional *Consulate*, with Bonaparte at its head.

THE CONSULATE.
NOVEMBER 1799-MAY 1804.

I. The New Constitution (Constitution of the Year VIII).

1. *Sieyès's Plan:*—Lists of notability,—the legislative body,—the Council of State,—the Tribunate,—the Senate,—the *Grand Électeur Proclamateur*,—the Consuls.

2. Debate on this in committee,—Sieyès's hope,—Bonaparte's course.

3. *The Constitution* as adopted,—its spirit and main features,—its immediate and remote results.

II. The New Government.

1. Bonaparte's relations to it.
2. Character of Cambacérès,—of Lebrun.

III. Conciliation.

General moderation in policy,—baits held out to Republicans and Royalists,—the coinage,—appointments of Talleyrand and Fouché,—treatment of the Church,—appointments to the public bodies.

IV. Reorganization.

1. Excellent choice of subordinates.
2. Finances,—public works,—the code, and Bonaparte's part in it.

V. General Progress towards Despotism.

1. Bonaparte's early declarations ("Three months of dictatorship to save the Republic"),—his immediate vio-

lation of the new constitution by "anticipating the popular will."

2. Centralization of power,—creation of special tribunals,—the police.

3. Caresses for the Church,—letter to the King of England,—the *Concordat*.

4. Residence at the Tuileries,—splendor,—changes in phraseology ("subject" for "citizen" in treaties). Suppression of the liberties of the press,—undermining and breaking down of the Tribunate. The Legion of Honor.

VI. Dealings with Europe.

General policy,—extortion practiced upon smaller powers,—Hamburg as a typical example,—use of peace to Bonaparte.

VII. Military Affairs.

1. Necessity of war to Bonaparte's policy.

2. Suppression of insurrections in La Vendée and in Brittany.

3. Italian campaign,—the "reserve camp",—passage of the Alps,—Marengo [14 June 1800]. Loss of Egypt. Moreau's victory at Hohenlinden.

4. Peace of Lunéville [February 1801]. Peace of Amiens [March 1802].

VIII. The Consulate for Ten Years and for Life.

1. Manner of the choice.

2. The expedition to Santo Domingo [March 1802],—major and minor motives for it,—the Army of the Rhine, treatment of Toussaint L'Ouverture as typical.

3. Revelations of Bonaparte's intentions,—rupture with England [May 1803].

IX. Opposition in France.

1. The two opposing parties,—explosion of the Rue St. Nicaise,—Bonaparte's incapacity for constitutional ideas exemplified in his treatment of guiltless Republicans.

2. Royalist plots,— Cadoudal,— Pichegru,— example made of the Duc d'Enghien.

X. The Close of the Consulate.

1. "Consular majesty",—preparations for an addition to Bonaparte's power,—effects of plots,—addresses of public bodies,—Carnot.

2. Proclamation of *the Empire* [May 1804].

THE FIRST EMPIRE.

I. FROM THE PROCLAMATION OF THE EMPIRE TO THE TREATY OF TILSIT.

MAY 1804-JULY 1807.

I. The First Development of Cæsarism.

1. The alliance with the Papacy,—recapitulation of Bonaparte's diplomacy with the Papal government.

2. The coronation [2 Dec. 1804],—revelations of character in it (citations from Bourrienne and Bausset). The coronation in Italy [26 May 1805],—the iron crown.

II. The War of the Third Coalition.

1. *Campaign of 1805:*—The flotilla in the English Channel,—sudden turning against Austria and Russia,—Ulm [17 Oct.],—peculiar exhibition of Napoleon's character at the Ulm capitulation,—Vienna,—Austerlitz [2 Dec.],—treaty of Presburg [26 Dec.],—end of the Holy Roman Empire.

2. Trafalgar [21 Oct. 1805]. Death of Pitt [23 Jan. 1806].

III. The War of the Fourth Coalition.

1. Growth of anti-French feeling in Prussia,—effect of Napoleon's diplomacy in aggravating this,—effect of the execution of Palm,—difficulties of Prussia as to territory and as to organization and command of armies.

2. The outbreak,—Jena [14 Oct. 1806],—condition of the Prussian monarchy after Jena.

3. The Berlin decrees [21 Nov. 1806],—their effect on international law. Treatment of Queen Louise,—revenge for this in 1871,—treatment of sundry officials,—Napoleon's trickery and deception.

4. Eylau [8 Feb. 1807] and Friedland [14 June],—significance of the battle of Eylau. Treaty of Tilsit [July 1807],—germs of political evil and international trouble in that treaty.

THE FIRST EMPIRE.

II. FROM THE TREATY OF TILSIT TO THE CONFERENCE AT ERFURT.

JULY 1807-SEPTEMBER 1808.

I. The New Growth of Imperial Institutions.

1. Organic law of the year XII,—the great officers of state,—the Marshals,—forms and ideas borrowed from olden empires.

2. The claim to the succession of Charlemagne,—curious statement of this by Napoleon, and striking developments of it.

3. New growth of the Legion of Honor,—new nobility,—the comical side of these new creations.

II. The Napoleonic European Feudal System.

The kingdom of Italy,—the Confederation of the Rhine, grand fiefs,—great vassals,—the remaining monuments of this in France.

III. The Napoleonic Internal Administration.

1. Public works,—Lanfrey's criticism.
2. The *Code Civil*.
3. Literature and science,—their decay,—historical parallels.

IV. Napoleonic Dealings with Liberties.

Chronic misapprehension of English liberty, and consequences of this. Suppression of the Tribunate. The

plébiscite. Dealings with journalism,—with courts of justice.

V. Napoleonic External Relations.

Peculiarities of Napoleon's diplomacy,—its shifting character,—cause of this in Napoleon's personal want of truth,—high-handed methods,—theatrical methods,—mingling in it of Italian and French characteristics,—Bourrienne's statement of Napoleon's formula,—warlike use of peaceful negotiations.

VI. Napoleonism approaching Culmination.

1. The break with the Papacy,—entrance into Portugal,—into the Ionian Islands,—into Naples.

2. Intrigues in Spain,—abdication of the Spanish King in favor of Napoleon,—accession of Joseph Bonaparte,—the effect on Europe. Specimens of the flatteries lavished on Napoleon.

VII. The First Great Check.

The Spanish uprising,—reception of Joseph in Spain,—the court,—the people,—the clergy,—French dealings with the Inquisition,—general summary. The siege of Saragossa,—Palafox,—capitulations of Baylen [July 1808] and Cintra [August 1808],—effect of these disasters upon European feeling.

THE FIRST EMPIRE.

III. FROM THE CONFERENCE AT ERFURT TO THE INVASION OF RUSSIA.

SEPTEMBER 1808-JUNE 1812.

I. The Conference at Erfurt.

1. Difficulties arising from the treaty of Tilsit,—their complication with the Spanish difficulty.

2. Sketch of the Erfurt conference,—apotheosis of Napoleon and humiliation of European royalty,—double purpose accomplished by Napoleon at this conference.

II. Napoleon's Personal Demonstration against Spain.

Intervention of England in the Peninsula,—England sees what Napoleon will not see,—one grand motive imbedded in Napoleon's meaner motives during the struggle in the Peninsula. Success of Napoleon,—failure of his generals,—his return to France.

III. The Fifth Coalition.

1. Austrian preparations for war,—causes of this,—wrangle over it,—insurrection of the Tyrol,—tardiness of Austria.

2. Vigor of Napoleon,—his genius in transmuting great faults of his generals into master-strokes,—Eckmühl [22 April 1809],—Aspern [21 May],—Wagram [6 July],—Lobau,—capitulation of Vienna,—treaty of Vienna [14 Oct. 1809].

IV. Attempted Consolidation of Cæsarism.

1. Napoleon's plans for a new marriage,—Maria Louisa.
2. Dealings with the finances,—new dealings with the press.
3. The continental blockade,—Napoleon's own infractions of it.

V. Ominous Change in the Spirit of France.

1. Change in the ideas of the people,—loss of convictions.
2. Change in the spirit of the army,—Erckmann-Chatrian's pictures. Sketch of Napoleon's minor methods with the people and the army,—bulletins,—speeches,—recognition of services.
3. Change in the spirit of the great military leaders,—beginning of estrangement between Napoleon and his older officers.
4. Change in the person of Napoleon.

THE FIRST EMPIRE.

IV. FROM THE INVASION OF RUSSIA TO THE ABDICATION OF NAPOLEON.

JUNE 1812-APRIL 1814.

I. The War with Russia.

1. Its causes,—Napoleon's combination of continental powers for the invasion,—the conscription in France and its effects.

2. Summary of events,—fancy and fact regarding the burning of Moscow,—significant relics of the French invaders now in the Kremlin.

3. The retreat,—its result upon European opinion,—the Malet conspiracy at Paris,—Napoleon at the Tuileries,—his requiem over his Russian army.

II. Sketch of French Domination in Germany.

Napoleon's maxim regarding the support of armies,—the practical application of this,—Davout and Bourrienne as types,—the execution of Palm.

III. The Uprising in Germany.

1. Significant action of General Yorck on the retreat from Moscow,—course of the king of Prussia.

2. German feeling, — the *Tugendbund*, — Körner, — Arndt,—Staps,—Schill,—the work of Stein and Hardenberg.

IV. New Invasion of Germany.

The new conscription in France and its results,—the first battles,—effect of the changed spirit of the French

and German armies,—the interview between Napoleon and Metternich at Dresden,—Leipzig [18, 19 Oct. 1813].

V. The Invasion of France.

1. The conference of Châtillon [Feb. 1814],—determination of Napoleon.

2. Brilliancy of his efforts,—a great plan not carried out,—Paris taken [31 March 1814].

3. Action of the legislative bodies,—abdication of Napoleon [11 April 1814],—intrigues,—Napoleon at Elba.

THE RESTORATION.

APRIL 1814–JULY 1830.

I. First Restoration of the Bourbons.

1. The Treaty of Paris [May 1814],—losses of France in territory,—intrigues regarding a new government in France,—Talleyrand and Fouché,—feeling of the Emperor Alexander regarding a Bourbon restoration.

2. Accession of Louis XVIII,—his character,—the "Charter",—royalist mistakes and absurdities,—Dupont Minister of War,—the Holy Alliance,—Congress of Vienna [1814-15],—state of society.

II. The Hundred Days.

1. Re-entrance of Napoleon into Europe,—his landing at Cannes [1 March 1815],—his progress,—Ney,—flight of Louis XVIII,—action of the Congress of Vienna.

2. The "Hundred Days" [March–June 1815],—the new conscription,—the war,—the battle of Waterloo [18 June 1815],—Napoleon's second abdication [22 June],—his flight,—his surrender,—his life at St. Helena.

III. Second Restoration of the Bourbons.

1. Return of Louis XVIII,—France still further reduced in territory.

2. Reign of Louis XVIII,—general reactionary character of the time,—assassinations,—massacres in the south of France,—executions,—the *Concordat*,—arbitrary acts,—death of Louis XVIII [1825].

IV. Charles X.

Character of Charles X,—his inferiority to Louis,—some features of his early history,—his coronation,—his reign [1825-1830],—state of society.

V. The Reaction in Full Bloom.

Growth of the reaction in literature under the Restoration,—Chateaubriand,—Lamennais,—De Maistre,—the Congregation,—societies affiliated with the Jesuits,—government action in politics and religion.

VI. Revival of the Spirit of the Revolution.

1. This revival in literature,—Béranger,—Paul-Louis Courier,—Victor Hugo,—Thiers's History of the Revolution,—lectures of Guizot, Villemain, and Cousin.

2. *The July Revolution:*—Action regarding the legislative body and the liberty of the press,—the outbreak [27 July 1830],—the three days,—Charles X driven from the throne,—the provisional government,—the Duke of Orleans comes to the throne as Louis Philippe, King of the French.

LOUIS PHILIPPE.

AUGUST 1830–FEBRUARY 1848.

I. Louis Philippe.

His early history,—some leading traits of his character,—deterioration of some of these, especially kingcraft and thrift.

II. General Difficulties in Administration at this Period.

Conflicting theories, expectations, sects, parties, and factions,—mania for position,—popular ignorance.

III. Special Difficulties of Louis Philippe's Administration.

1. The charter restriction of the suffrage,—characters of Guizot, Thiers, and other leaders,—death of the Duke of Bourbon,—the cholera,—insurrections of Paris and Lyons.

2. Republican attempts,—socialist attempts,—legitimist attempts, — Bonapartist attempts, — Louis Napoleon at Strasbourg and Boulogne,—Polish attempts,—attempts at assassination.

3. Unreason on both sides,—professional revolutionists,—Blanqui and Barbès as types,—the Archbishop of Paris on the cholera, and the Archbishop of Besançon on railways.

4. *Current of Literature Undermining the Throne:*—Michelet's "History of France"—Lamartine's "History

of the Girondists",—Thiers's "Consulate and Empire",
—Louis Blanc's writings,—journalism.

5. Difficulties of Anglican constitutional government on the continent of Europe, and especially in France.

6. Death of the Duke of Orleans,—difficulties abroad,—recognition by European powers,—Poland, Holland, and Belgium.

IV. Character of his Reign.

1. *Its Better Side:*—Efforts at constitutional rule,—choice of ministers,—moderation,—common sense (citation from Guizot's "Mémoires"),—character of the court,—public works,—social amelioration,—English alliance,—the war in Algiers, (*a*) as a training school for soldiers, (*b*), as the forerunner of colonization,—common sense methods,—the Robert-Houdin example.

2. *Its More Doubtful Side:*—The Paris fortifications,—their double purpose,—expected and real results,—dealings with the Duchess of Berri,—influencing of legislation,—accumulation of wealth by the King,—contemporary opinion of him.

V. The Guizot Administration.

"Smart" policy,—attempts to pet the English monarch and cheat English statesmen,—loss of the English alliance,—peaceful policy,—use made of this by Thiers and others,—the basis of suffrage,—use made of this.

VI. The Revolution of 1848.

The cry made for reform,—the banquets,—stubbornness of Guizot,—suddenness of the Revolution of 1848,—Lagrange,—abdication of the King [Feb. 1848],—character of this revolution,—of sterile revolutions in general.

THE REPUBLIC OF 1848 AND THE SECOND EMPIRE.

I. The Provisional Government and Second Republic.

Difficulties in the capital and in the country,—Lamartine's efforts,—Louis Blanc's efforts,—organization of labor,—the national workshops,—struggles with destructives,—Proudhon's phrase,—the Brea murder as typical,—Cavaignac.

II. Transition to the Empire.

Louis Napoleon's "profession of faith" on entering France (citations from "Les Murailles Révolutionnaires"),—phrases skillfully made and spread,—examples of the effect of phrase-mongering in France. Election of Louis Napoleon to the presidency,—the conspiracy,—the *coup d'état*,—statements of Kinglake and of Bishop Coxe,—treatment of Thiers and others,—harshness to republicans and socialists,—the "Deportations." Inevitable approach of "the man on horseback."

III. The Second Empire.

1. *Diplomatic and Military Successes:*—Title taken,—tone towards foreign powers,—Eastern question,—the Holy Places,—English alliance and Crimean war,—mutual endearments of French and English sovereigns.

2. *Administrative Successes:*—Splendor given to great cities,—strategic objects,—Haussmann,—the finances,—Fould,—the national loan,—material progress of France.

3. Lines of policy relied upon to win the middle classes,—the proletariate,—the liberals,—the reactionists,—the people in general,—significance of the Italian war and the treaty of Villafranca,—attempts to ally Cæsarism with liberalism,—" Life of Cæsar,"—Duruy,—decentralization,—losing of shackles upon the press.

IV. Weakening of the Imperial Power.

1. The invasion of Mexico and its results,—war between Austria and Prussia and its results,—supposed culmination of the imperial power in the events which led to its downfall.

2. Results of the increased freedom of the press,—Bohemianism,—Rochefort and *La Lanterne*,—Pierre Bonaparte and Victor Noir.

3. Results of increased freedom of speech,—the Thiers speeches,—the Ollivier government.

V. Decline and Collapse of the Second Empire.

1. French awakening after the battle of Sadowa,—progress of evil relations with Prussia,—war and anti-war parties,—the Empress Eugénie,—Thiers.

2. Outbreak of war [19 July 1870],—utter breaking down of the material, mental, and moral strength of France,—revelations in the Tuileries papers,—Lebœuf,—the Prussian triumph.

3. The Thiers government and the Commune,—" Communal " rule (citations from certain recent publications, especially " La Fin de la Bohême " in the *Revue des Deux Mondes*),—one good result: collapse of a superstition regarding the Parisian mob.

VI. The Third Republic.

The Wallon constitution,—Gambetta,—presidency of Thiers,—of Mac Mahon,—the Jules Simon and Fortou episodes,—the Grévy presidency,—the Freycinet policy and its results,—industrialism *vs.* " glory."

www.ingramcontent.com/pod-product-compliance
Lightning Source LLC
Chambersburg PA
CBHW030310170426
43202CB00009B/945